Come And See

Clem Suder

therightpathclemsuderbooks.com

Come
And
See

CLEM SUDER

508 West 26th Street

KEARNEY, NE 68848

402-819-3224

info@medialiteraryexcellence.com

Come And See

Copyright © 2023 Clem Suder

ISBN (Paperback): 978-1-958082-57-7

ISBN (Ebook): 978-1-958082-56-0

Printed in the United States of America

CONTENTS

INTRODUCTION

This book is my third book about what I saw and experienced. It is also a witness to the way I was prepared for it. I hope that it will open your mind to new possibilities in understanding even though, it will require a perspective that is not so judgmental, and truly the acceptance of a child not to challenge things because you were told something else and taught it as truth but were told when you find something that it fails to explain, it is your understanding that is the problem. The truth does not change it is one way you can prove to yourself what is true. Our understanding of it and the perspective we choose can vary but the truth and the results never vary. As you proceed through this book, I hope my explanation of the reasoning and my conclusions will help you experience it as well, but, I can only hope it will cause you to seek and ask the father the creator of all things to see the answer as he showed me he will you, with things you understand because of your choice and past. What you give power too has power in your life it is the completion of the love and mercy God gives each of us. If I could I wish to have everyone experience the feelings and understanding it gives.

Much of what I discuss in this book may seem unbelievable, however we are dealing with the creator, who created all for his purpose and therefore everything must work to accomplish that purpose. We may not like it, but it does not change what will be. there are references to scripture I do not give you chapter and verse. This is not about someone else said about how they interacted with the creator of all, but of how and what he showed me. I am not here to start a new religion of man; I am here to show that in many ways and many different understandings still serve the purpose of creation. I know there are many who would say because of what they say and been told there is only one way to be saved but these are the same people that say he died to pay for your freedom to sin, instead of he lived to show you that you could live and be the children of God you were meant to be and that the first death cannot hold you. He did not say I am the end, but I am the light and the way. His path is supposed to be your path but you think the path should be free and require nothing of you. To this I will reply as he did to his disciples, in the end many will come to me saying Lord, lord, and I will look at them and say, "why do you call me lord, and do not what I said? I don't know you." The book is really about what he and the prophets with sight saw themselves not what others say they meant. It is based in their direct words.it really is the retelling of the words of Jesus because he never quoted man's religion, Jesus spoke of the father's grace and love for us.

The time is upon each to decide what they choose for themselves we like to say judgement day, however since you are your own judge of yourself by what you say and do, the concept of being held on one day shows it is not the method of the father who wants to save all. There is no day except in the minds of the religious who want to blame others and say others judge them. The fact is mercy requires that you allow the values of the individual to be honored, so if you choose to be apart you will be, not because someone else chose it for you but, because by your thoughts words and actions you chose it. So I tell you as Jesus told the young lady accused of adultery, go and sin no more. Are you ready to pick up your cross and follow me? Do you have the peace and certainty he had, it took me seven years to get past the fear and understand how.

CHAPTER 1

Come And See
Who Am I

I know you would be curious to find out who am I that can talk of these things. When I was a child growing up around Cleveland Ohio my family was going through a divorce. So, there were not much in the way of true peace in the house. To be honest I don't remember that much at that time.at any rate my mother moved out and we were left with my father. I really don't know much about him since he was always working. He did hire babysitters but being children who did not want them but wanted our mother instead and there were four of us we were probably a hand full. Prior to that my older sister and I had been playing in the yard and this couple used to stop and invite us to go with them to Sunday school. It was a different time then and our mother was ok with them taking us to their church. Since we did not go to church as a family, and I don't honestly remember it being discussed much. I would say we were not from a particularly religious family; however, I knew some of my aunts were very religiously motivated. To a young child it seemed that their religion made them angry and judgmental. So, they were committed to their understanding. I certainly knew better than to seek to discuss it with them since I really did not know them that well. I just remember what seemed like anger in their eyes. At the time since it was me and my sister going, I went to Sunday school. I don't remember what denomination the church was. But I did hear about Jesus and wondered why I had sensed so much anger around religion. It seemed like he did not talk much about it to me. As time went by, we were probably creating to much discontent for the live in babysitters, so my older sister and I were sent to live with my fathers' parents. It was a farm and very different from the city we were used too, but there were lots of fun things we could do although we shouldn't have. But nevertheless, we did. Our grandfather had helped raise many of his grandchildren, but he was not young, and our grandmother usually was busy around the house, so I don't remember talking much to her about anything that was not pressing at that moment. We never had spiritual discussions with either that I can recall still, the Sunday school had started me thinking about God. Which was quite an accomplishment because I was a typical boy and did not seem to spend a lot of time thinking in philosophical terms. I was too busy having fun with things I shouldn't have been doing like taunting the bull and swinging from rope in the barn over the hay. But while I was there, I was with family so I did not think about what would be. one day as I was playing in the creek it felt like I was playing with someone it is hard to put into words those feelings just that somehow, I knew I was not alone. But there was no threat I could tell, and I felt like we just played till I got called back to the house, I remember not wanting to go but when the grandparents called you did not keep them waiting for any length of time. I wanted to say good by to the friend that had been playing with me, but I could never see him only the light. At that time, I heard and felt inside that he said" I am with you always." I was confused but I had to go. I had learned enough that there are things you don't talk about this seemed like one of those because I didn't know where to take anyone to meet my playmate. still, I puzzled over the fact I never could clearly see them, and I heard them, but I felt what I heard. At any rate I was a child with my own fun agenda to get on with and it seemed best not to talk about it.

That was my first encounter with the unusual things in life, that I could not explain but knew what I had felt, and saw were real. That voice and feeling stuck with me for many years always seemingly in the back of my mind. It did not change my boyhood antics or my curiosity, but it was always there. I just assumed that's what it meant. As time went on and I grew older I learned more about the scriptures but always filtered by my feelings of what is real for me. Part of what I learned was about thousand-year-old prophecies, "I will be the father to the fatherless, "since I did not really know my father as I hope most people don't have to say it seemed to me he was talking to me at least that felt right. After all Jesus said when asked how do we pray? "Our father who art in heaven", he did not say my father but our father which meant he is one with us. And he wants us to be like he was.

As I went through life, I tried to always listen to that little voice inside it kept me out of a lot of trouble, but it also allowed me to choose what may not have been the best choice, but it was the choice I made without ever intentionally setting out to harm or hurt anyone. It is an important part of who you are and what you seek because it is the foundation of how you establish your values.

Unless you understand that the true nature of what you value comes from within you will never understand why Jesus said" it is not what enters you that corrupts you but what comes from you." In this manner even though I was not going to any seminary the words of the scriptures came to life in me. That is not to say I was perfect I made my mistakes and paid the consequences for them thankfully they were small and therefore the lessons while memorable were also not fatal. I was gifted with an extraordinary mind great memory and problem-solving skills learning was easy and remembering was so automatic. If I were interested in something I could immerse myself in it and keep up with what was going on around me. I remember when I was in middle school the teacher seemed to call on me whenever they wanted to talk about what we had learned the semester before, and I was reading a book at my desk jack London or along those lines. But even though I was reading something totally not related I could almost always give them the answer they were looking for. All of this was to prepare me to be able to see. My mother met and married a police officer, jailor in the city of Cleveland, he was short tempered and very brutal when it came to physical punishment probably a biproduct of his raising and the world he lived in. I would like to think the brutality was not common. My mother would come into my room at night and pull back the covers and weep because of the bruising. I tried repeatedly to tell her it was ok, and I did not feel it. But I don't know if she ever really heard or believed me. In this manner I learned about violence and the ways it impacts the world around. I came to the realization that the best thing for me was to stay occupied outside the home, so I got my first job at thirteen working as a busboy in a restaurant. In order to be able to stay and work there as much as I possibly could I was determined to be the best at what I did so they would want me to be there. In order to do that I listened and learned from everyone to be better and solve some of the issues they had and complained about. This continued in every job and opportunity I got because the more I knew how to do well the more people would want me to be there. While I know now that child labor laws were not enforced as rigidly then as now, the reality that I never complained about the hours or refused to work them helped me go under the radar. That and I was always big for my age it was not uncommon for me to be working with older and sometimes college age people and because for the most part my interactions with them was strictly work it never became a problem I knew of. However, the maturity of some of the waitresses raised my awareness of physical desire probably more than someone who primarily interacts with people their own age. This became apparent to me when I was probably fourteen and I would go to church occasionally on Sundays to check out the girls in their tight-fitting dresses. It was at one of these days that I was sitting in the balcony watching some particularly well-endowed girls toward the front of the church when I happened to glance at the big cross which hung above the altar and it was like from the center of the cross a bright light emerged and seemed to engulf me again I felt this and wanted to look around and shout out to those around me, did you see that? But upon looking at them it became apparent they had not. So again, I kept it to myself and did not talk about this incident to anyone I can remember however I might have talked about it to my sister although I am sure I left out the part of checking out the girls. To say the least this along with the other seemingly supernatural events I had experienced was making me wonder what it means, but in keeping with the social accepted norms I kept it to myself and wondered. Since it did not make me behave in any unacceptable ways or cause me to think anything that I don't think any early teenage boy thinks about, I basically dropped it at least, from anything I would discuss with anyone because I had no idea why such things should happen to anyone and perhaps, I hoped it was my imagination. But I am sure because it made me wonder and try to find answers for myself why these things would be important enough to be brought so strongly to my attention. Again, lessons that while at the time I did not understand embedded in such away as to be considered later.by the time I was sixteen I could do any job in the restaurant and run the kitchen in the toughest rush's and do it smoothly. Many people were happy for me to be there for any rush including bar crowd. There were times I would go to work after school on Friday and work and cover for people who called off and would take breaks between rushes to sleep in the storeroom. There were occasions when I would go to work on Friday evening and my sister would pick me up and bring me home Sunday afternoons. It was certainly a different time in our country. I was not forced to do this it was better than the potential for violence with my stepfather. I remember one night he and my mother were arguing and he punched her in the mouth and broke some of her teeth she would not let me get between them to protect her. But I never forgot that and thought someday I would be able to treat him the way he treated others. So, I enlisted in the marine corps when I was turning eighteen the regimen was different but not that particularly rough for me since I had lived with him, and he was worse than any drill instructor and more dangerous than anything they would put us through. All of this was part of the preparation for what was to come in my life. Because I had been so protected from feeling so much hurt and I had not followed the normal path I think I was emotionally immature and looked for love in faces of people that I chose instead of seeing how they chose to love. It would cause me to make some of the worst mistakes in my life.

There was much I needed to learn still for all the scriptures and their meaning to be clear to me. One of the things that I was not aware of was, in my mind, I was building this fantasy perfect world without knowing what it would take to get there. There were so many questions because of the past experiences. And so much more to come. I remember coming home on leave one Christmas and they had bought these blow-up boxing gloves, of course she pleaded that my stepfather and I put them on and show her how they were supposed to work. I knew it was a bad idea, but I couldn't resist. By this time, I was a big boy and a marine in shape, it was not long before he was getting frustrated, and we did not continue thank God. I am glad we quit because I was worried it would get bloody and this time not mine. But it too registered with me subconsciously. It was at once rewarding and disappointing because I did not want to hurt anyone even though they had hurt others so. I felt I could have easily hurt him. I was home to see my girlfriend who eventually became my wife and the mother of my sons. Unfortunately, I still did not know enough to observe all things and see what is there before me. Again, a biproduct of my judgement without understanding.

There was so much I was yet to understand the things like the Tibetan monks who literally wall themselves up to achieve a transcendental state. Hoping to become one with the universe. Or the lengths people will go to enforce their religious ideas on others. Along with the actual meaning of true value and how it is used here to control and limit freedom. The fact that that coupled with the meaning of creation will cause the destruction of value. All of this was yet to be shown me. I got out of the marines and went back to the restaurant business this time working for the franchise office which meant travelling around to other stores to teach how to setup and run kitchens and consequently work with the wait staff as well. I had by now gotten married and the long hours and travel were difficult as well as the pay was insufficient. A friend of my wife worked at a university and told us about a job opening there. I applied and got hired it was fixing equipment in the dental medical and nursing schools primarily dental. I worked therefore a few years, and it was better pay and eight to five but the pay was not enough to raise a family on. One of my coworkers who had done this work for a private company suggested I check into that because they pay so much better. I did and got hired as a technician for them I was making more but the hours were certainly not eight to five which led to many arguments about the hours and eventually to accusations of infidelity. This was something I could not stand most of my life I had been beaten and accused of things I did not do and in my mind, this was something I could not permit anymore. So, it ended in divorce, and I was determined not to allow my children to be used as a tool to harm me because they would be harmed. So, because of my faith and commitment to God as I knew him, I asked him to protect them and kept tabs on them without allowing their mother to use them as a tool. At that time, you did not stand much of a chance against a woman in small town courts so initially it was not found in my favor but as the boys grew older, they wanted to come live with me and eventually I did get custody of my younger son. I continued in my field and eventually got promoted to regional services manager in the southeast united states I had locations in six states, so I was back to travelling without really eight to five type work. But I really liked what I did and part of what I did was teaching diagnostics and repair work to tech from other regions as well as my own. This type of work because of the travel and hours is not very supportive to a social or romantic life but I interacted and met people easily so while they were generally not long term, I did have relationships. One year after my yearly check up my doctor told me I had high blood pressure and prescribed me medication I did not know this type of medication does not help your body do what it is supposed to it replaces what your body does so you must always take it and your body does not get stronger itself. Well, I took it for about a month and went on one of my weeklong trips through the region and ran out of medication on Tuesday I didn't think much about it and figured I would get it Saturday when I got home. I got home late Friday night and went to bed didn't feel good got up to get aspirin and evidently passed out and fell down the hardwood stairs resulting in a traumatic brain injury. My son found me the next day the Ems came but did not take me to the hospital, evidently, I knew the president was bush but did not know who my son was. The next day he told me we were going to McDonalds, but he took me to the hospital, and they kept me there for quite a while. My son had moved back up north, and they would not let me out of the hospital without a full-time caregiver. And so it was that a woman I had only dated a few times became my caregiver and friend. Her family basically adopted me and so they became my family here. As for me I had to start the whole process of finding myself from what for all appearances was a zombie state. It took about seven years because I really had no short-term memory and very compromised long-term memory to get to the state of after reading in the bible that Jesus told the Sanhedrin the ruling party of the Jewish state as his only defense, he said I require mercy I do not require sacrifice, if you knew the difference you would know where my authority comes from. I realized I really did not know the difference so even in my incomplete state I asked God to show me and teach me the difference. This led to one afternoon after many days of trying to know the difference and asking God to teach me the difference one afternoon while I was laying on my bed I heard and felt I saw a hand and heard that old voice say "Come and See" so I thought I took his hand, and the journey began.

CHAPTER 2

Come And See, The Journey

And so it began, it felt as if I had gotten up off the bed, but my body was still there. I had only felt this once before in a hospital when I worked at the university, I had been put in the hospital because I had mononucleosis strep throat and allergies. All at once and I recall hearing on the intercom inhalation therapy room 216 code blue. I remember I was upset because I thought I was in an isolation room, I looked down and there were a bunch of people working on somebody, the next thing I know is the next day and the doctor told me I had flatlined the night before. So, it felt like I did then complete yet without a real body. Then it seemed like we were going through a tunnel, and we seemed to stop at different time and places usually when something particularly brutal or sad was happening and I asked my guide could they see me usually I got no reply. Then it was back in the tunnel to the next stop. Some of the stops I knew from history books for instance I think it was in

Saipan during the second world war and there were mothers throwing their children off of cliffs and then jumping to their deaths after them. I remember my guide seemed to have tears in his eyes as did i. then through the prisoner of war camps in the civil war the prisoner of war ships in the revolutionary war, the wars in Africa, ad Jerusalem back through time even Sodom and Gomorrah where it looked like a nuclear blast. Back through time Cain and Abel. All the way back to the tree of knowledge of good and Evil. Then the next stop was what looked to me like a quaint modern English village with the neatly manicured lawns and thatch roofs people out doing yard work or just talking but this time they seemed to see us and were willing to talk with us. I did not really know what to say so I listened and heard them talking about helping each other and the neighbors, I was puzzled and could not resist asking them if they knew me, the Answer kind of shocked me they said of course you have always been here. That was shocking to me yet somehow felt right. Just the way they dealt with each other the genuine concern for each other as themselves. It made me feel like this must be heaven. After that I expected to see palaces and instead, I found my self in a place that was seemingly without borders with what looked to me like universes stretched out before me. And I felt and seemingly heard "I am that I am, I am the Alpha and the omega" it made me want to fall on my face with wonder and fear. Yet it had not been said with anger more like a father talking to a son. It began as a feeling I could go anywhere and see everything, and it made sense to me. All the stops on the way here began to sort themselves out before my eyes. What had been and why it had been. Because God was showing me all things. When he told Moses you cannot even conceive of me much less name me, because what you name you think you can define you cannot conceive of me so you can't name me tell Pharoah I am sent you. All of this and so much more he showed me. I am all energy in forms you can't grasp it is the energy working within me that created the matter when I called all things into being. Each thing complete with all that was required for it to be. the energy you call life from me and in all things in levels you can't know or define yet. All energy the maker of matter and antimatter. The energy that goes through yet can do no damage and the energy that goes through and when contacted by matter results in annihilation. All serve me and my purpose which is I always get greater I require that things work to always create greater or are removed in the process of making greater. The tree you saw the knowledge of good and evil is the living embodiment of that overall objective it is the primary rule of nature itself. All things work to increase because I always increase. That is what good is, evil divides in order to define what good comes from the increase. It is always less than and just a portion if you choose it you receive less than in other words you lose some. consider what you saw when you first got in this place. A huge empty room with the universes spread out on the floor before you. Look again and see as I see, it was then as if I were floating in space not with the universes spread out on the floor but all around above and below me. This is to show you the truth of your vision it has been eight years since your vision the universes spread out on the floor made you wonder. But you are writing as you were called to do. Just as the universes were called into being and therefore everything that is required must be there. What you need to see is always there, but will you look through my eyes or yours? In the beginning you were in me, and I am in you, and we are one. All that is required for you to do what I called you to do will be there. Think now after that lesson of life all are called into being they have a choice either increase the value of that gift of being or separate yourself. Separate you can never increase the value all things have to be there to increase the value. Consider a coin it has multiple sides and was created for a purpose if any of the sides or the purpose are removed it can not be a coin. Its value is gone. The coin outside of the purpose is just matter it has no life the same is for those called into being who choose to ignore or turn their back on the purpose of their creation or who choose to be only one side of the coin never able to be anything else or fulfill their purpose but always knowing they had a purpose. They are really in what we could call hell unable to do or interact yet knowing they were supposed to. So too will it be for those who choose to be one side and separate themselves from me and their purpose which was to make things greater as I am always greater.

With each lesson I see more of what as been and begin to know why it was. As well as understand why things are the way they are today. We live in a world divided and we allow those division of men to generate our judgement system which really is our value system. We give other people and society the right to rule our lives in spite of the fact what they do removes value and truth. We do not see the world through our father's eye we see the flat universes that could not ever actually exist. Our whole understanding of how to be we allow others to dictate to us because we don't want to be alone not realizing if we separate ourselves from our true purpose, we have lost all value. It made me think of the people I had spoken with in heaven, they never considered anything apart from but always the value of together and whole. We think in terms of what we see not in terms of what must exist for anything to be complete or real. We see one side of a wall but think nothing of the fact that the other sides must exist as well or there is no wall. The same with the concept of good and evil we see one or the other and don't understand one is only real if the other is part of it because we could not even define either without the other. However, like the people in heaven know both sides exist but only choose to use the sides that will accomplish the purpose making it greater. Consequently, we think heaven would not require anything the fact is that would remove the purpose of creation and it is when we work together to accomplish that purpose that heaven can exist.

It was during this vision I began to see how the people I knew would not want to hear these things because they challenge all of the traditional teachings they have been raised by. Like me they would have seen the universes flat because they have always been taught that the singular point of view is the way to see all things. With this in mind I again felt fear and asked father, why are you showing me all these things? To which he said tell them what you see. I said father they will not believe me I am not a religious leader or a political leader, I am an old man from Georgia. Everyone you have sent to tell them these things they kill. Why me? He said I called you for this and it will be done fear not. Everyone who is born will die but those who do what they were called for will not suffer the second death. Why should you be concerned with people who can give you the first death and not fear the one who can give you the second death which is you by turning yourself from me and my purpose. I hid Jesus for years from Harrod even after I told them he was coming. I sent him to a time without worldwide communication yet made his message worldwide since I send you. You will accomplish my purpose and just as Jesus lived to show them the truth of his message you will be in heaven as you were told when you were there you have always been there. I am the beginning and the end you were in me, and I am in you, and we are one. To whom much is given much is expected and you have seen heaven and been with me. We know people will divide because they do not see they see the splinter in their neighbor's eye but cannot see the beam in their own eye. Do not fear you have seen already. Come and see what will be.

At this point I was able to see the world and how they were already setting up the abomination which causes desolation, which is socialism, because it removes true value and removes the reward for making things greater, or the purpose of all creation. It relies on the confiscation of value and redistributing it to who they want to. It removes the incentive to producing increase.

CHAPTER 3

Come And See, The Wonders As I Saw Them

All the things I saw on this journey was not only through my eyes but the eye of my spirit which sees and feels and acknowledges the truth. In every microsecond it seemed there was a wealth of knowledge given. Even when I did not see I knew. I saw and understood the messages and purpose for the messages as we progressed through mankind's journey to return to one. That is what it takes to have and share heaven, like the tree of knowledge of good and evil all must be there in order for it to exist but you only would ever choose to do those things which will raise the value of the gift God gives us which is life, but the life we know with our body is a portion to teach us to be able to accept and learn to do those things that are necessary to accomplish our purpose which is to make all greater. When men were faced with trying to create a form that would copy the creators work,

26

they needed to find a way to approximate worth. In order to achieve that they came up with the concept of money. It approximated what they thought your worth and feelings were worth. It is not real because our creator endowed each of thus with the freedom to determine for ourselves what something is true worth to them. Since no one else can feel exactly what you feel because you get to determine what and how much you will feel about anything the concept of money is flawed, which is why consumer confidence is tantamount to making it work. It did not start out by being backed by force but by something everyone wanted or needed. In order to regulate it society had to decide what they think it was worth and so began the decline of true value because they could not know the feelings of all the individuals only what each of them felt and since not everyone received true joy by all the things, they had to do allowing someone else do them worked good for some but removed value of what others did. So, in order to solve this problem, the threat of expulsion and eventually force was used to supplant or prop up consumer confidence. The way it is today is what they tell you. There was a time when the government was required to stockpile gold to provide physical confidence in the dollar, but they have worked around that in order to dictate what will give them power. If people really took time to understand what and how the concept of money really came about and worked, they would be more prepared to deal with issues of worth. Including the worth of experiencing heaven always not just after they have expired this portion of their life. As it is since they have been brought up with the understanding that it is the society that establishes worth, they can rarely deal with questions of true value. This is not new it has existed since the beginning of the need for the concept of money, and as a result When Jesus told the Sanhedrin he requires mercy, he did not require sacrifice, because it is a statement of true value that if they knew the difference they would know where his authority came from. It was a fact because to truly know the difference you must know God since he is the establisher of true value. Since true value is established within the individual the concept of how you use it properly becomes another place that the partial truth of society can corrupt the purpose of creation. Our words seldom have stability and are at the whim of society to continue to mean the same thing for long, so too with the concept of Mercy and Sacrifice. Yet it was this very understanding that I sought from the father that led me to everything. No wonder Jesus told them if they knew the difference, they would know god because true value comes from the individual freedom he gave us to provide worth to what we chose without regard to anyone else. It became one of the keys to social stabilization. So, if you did as Jesus did and challenge the way society in this case the Jewish church claimed authority even though you are telling the truth to silence you would require cutting you off in most cases the easiest way to do that is to have you killed. Because it still doesn't change the truth the message will eventually overpower the baseless lie. However, like all things there are many sides to consider and because all must be present for anything to exist there is partial truth connected to every lie or legend and there is partial lies that can be connected with what people perceive as truth. So, you must spell out the perspective and prove it to the individual in order to communicate the truth. You must show why it is the truth despite what lies that are there or connected. That is the responsibility of all of Gods children to test all things and see what they support. Is it bringing things back to one or does it divide and dismiss others. Understanding true value can only be done by you because each of you establishes what has true value to you and why. What society or social groups support is what they think you must value and if you don't there is something wrong with you. Since they can not really define or truthfully show how God only supports their view it is something that invariably will lead to their destruction so if they want to continue, they leave this alone even though they want to control and convince everyone in the group to accept what they tell you. Which is why under the best of circumstances which is you avoid all question of morality and faith and God because it will destroy the social structure. That is why most governments even monarchy must have periodic changes or the lose their authority to enough of the population to cause revolt. Some of them partial enough but left unaddressed can become military in nature.

Now I have tried to show you the nature of true value and how it is formed and supported. Let us consider the actual questioned things sacrifice and mercy. Please remember this is on an individual basis it is not on a social or community basis. It is statements about how and why things were created the way they were. And why I tell you I am not come to convert your church or society or social group I want to talk to you the individual the message I am showing you is for you individually from your father. I don't want to have you talk to anyone but our father and creator God himself. If you want to break this down and try its precepts in any of your life or history, please do you will see its true if you still don't understand talk to God yourself, he loves you and wants to hear from you. All that I have seen is yours the peace he gives me I give to you. You are a child of God no matter what you have done or failed to do he wants to hear from you not your priest or neighbor but because your feelings are in volved he must hear from you. Having told you where to source all of this let us consider mercy which Jesus said he requires. Worth is your feelings and what you devote yourself too. To increase it you must share it with someone who is capable to see the value you put in it and your commitment to it. Because it is ultimately what you want others can only give you what you seek as best, they can. This process of sharing and increasing the value is called mercy. It is about the increase of value or feelings which generally equivalates to joy. The increase of value of all things id=s what this creation is about. It is why each of us was given this portion to learn to do. So, when you have mercy on someone or something it is not about what you value, it is all about what they valued. Sometimes it can seem like a loss but because you are supposed to be sharing and increasing the value of what they felt it increases the value always. As an example, I will use the dead service people who died fighting to preserve our freedoms in this nation. Mercy requires that you appreciate understand and share their commitment to freedom for us our families and those yet to come. It was so valuable to them they gave their lives to preserve it. Jesus devotion to the father as he knew him was what he was trying to impart to all who would hear. Because it did not go along with the social desires he had to die. If people can understand and share his feelings about how he would as faithfully serve his father, then if you honored him and his words and sought to be like him his words and life had meaning they could not destroy no matter what they thought of him. I point out the same is true for those who gave their lives fighting for freedom. Since 1900 most if not all the wars were against socialist nations in one form or another. Today the people are electing socialist their forefathers and families fought against to run this nation. It turns what they gave their lives too into a sacrifice which means that what they felt and died for has no value, rather than raise the value of the gifts of their lives to preserve freedom people are throwing all that value away. That is what sacrifice does it throws away something of value to something that has no value or removes value. Because people don't know the difference and are willing to allow to not only redefine sacrifice, but they also think they are right. Again, I talk of the whole, the truth is there is loss if it ends up destroying what people gave their lives for it is loss. Consequently, you made their lives and deaths meaning less but because someone else tells you it is good until it completes the destruction of the freedom, they died for you will never realize the difference. That is why it is important for you to go to the father and not listen to what someone else says. His intent is clear and never changes.

Remember God always increases he never decreases; sacrifice is what men require because they know punishment not making things greater. In order to prove to them they are in charge you must suffer. God gave you what you have he does not want it to be taken or given unless it increases the good for all. If it serves good its mercy if it serves loss, it's sacrifice. Since Jesus used this as his only defense, I would say this understanding is vital. Yet of all the churches and denominations I have been to no one teaches this. Could it be that like the Sanhedrin who supposedly served the God of Abraham father of Jesus not known the difference? Unfortunately, most of the clergy I talk to today have very little clue what it meant even today. And yet he told them if they knew the difference, they would know whose authority he did what he did. Strange it is not spoken of more. And yet they teach sacrifice as good. It seems I heard somewhere in the end times they will treat lies as though they were true. Oh yeah revelations, since it ultimately does exactly the opposite of what the meaning of creation is I would hope people would learn through this and re reading the scriptures instead of seeing through their eyes see them through his, where the meaning of all and all that must be there become visible instead of one dimension.

Now perhaps you can see why so much of revelations is so unclear, and yet very descriptive of what has been happening. It is as I said and in most things value that is pivotal from knowing God to giving power to men, their churches and society, and social structures. To put them in their proper place I must deal with on other vital subject. Your judgement, and how it should relate to the world and the father.

I hope that as you read this you can feel or see as I did. It is hard for me to tell you what I saw because we tend to think of things one issue at a time. At least from one perspective at a time, when I saw this, it was as though everything was there and presented at once. Therefore, I have difficulty trying to deal with the issues as sides and try not to lose the purpose which is all. It is not the independent sides but the whole always with the purpose that is important. Because of that what seems like separate issues are one continuous truth, judgement is like that if you judge anything you do it from whatever perspective you choose and the reality that everyone can have a separate perspective is lost to you. Because they are really connected and hand in hand the truth is simple it is when we divide the truth that we run into problems. Because in truth everything must be there for anything to be the truth is very simple although like all things you can see perspectives, but it is the whole that is most important, remember what I said in all things there is the good which is all and when you divide it you get less than and that is evil. But both always must be there. It is because of this that when you judge you can only truly judge yourself because that is the only one you can see all the perspectives of and that is what will generate your feelings. The good news is what Jesus said judge not lest you be judged. And the way the father made all things with all that had to be in them for them to exist, you do not have to judge anything because it will judge itself by what it leads to or causes. If it leads to more it is good and will lead to more good if it is evil, it will divide and lead to loss. So, what you are really called to do is to observe and allow whatever it is or whoever it is to receive the consequences of what they did. That is truly mercy, not what you think but the results of what they said or did. You should now see the many things such as mercy and sacrifice, good and evil, judgement, even life itself you are given the ability to decide for yourself. If you give up that right to others or to society, you have given up the dominion God gave you. And that is what other men have been seeking since the beginning of time. It is why what is coming and happening now as well as what has already transpired is. And can not be changed for everyone each decides for themselves and must be held accountable for what they chose. Not because someone else accused them or said they did or thought they did. This is justice. True justice. You can try to blame others, but they had no authority other than what you gave them.

CHAPTER 4

Come And See, Power And Energy

Power, what men seek over each other but can only be granted when you allow it. As I have told you there are things I will challenge you to think about this is an example. When I was telling you about my journey I talked to you about the stops on the way. One of them was Saipan during World War 2 I talked about seeing mothers throwing their children off cliffs to their deaths and then jumping to their death. I also talked to you about how mercy is seeing how they value things and allowing them to. I mentioned that my guide had tears in his eyes as did I. now I understand it was not the deaths because Jesus proved the first death will happen to all, but they chose by what they did the second death is what they chose the loss of what could have been. Those women believed that what they did was required by their culture and showed amazing dedication that it took for them to do that. Our tears were because their culture taught them the emperor was a God. And in order to be viewed by other people what they did was required by men. It is a shame that people would believe anything like that. Again, what they chose to give power to. In fact, Germany was following the same path of following what other men told them was correct. It led to the death of millions, just to be acceptable to other men. All the pursuit of power. To be greater than others and more than them. And that millions allowed this is amazing. Both different types of socialist nations. the reason socialism is the abomination that causes desolation, socialism requires you allow society or other people to establish what your value is. it can only exist if it has someone's value to confiscate or steal. Part of their promise is the reduction of true productivity. It is this failure to create that will inevitably lead to desolation. Even though that society thinks there will always be someone they can force to produce what they need. You can now see what happens when people follow what others choose for them. All thinking they will receive for free. So, while it is mercy to allow them to choose what will destroy them it is also inevitable to destroy them. So even mercy does not negate the first death in fact choosing to follow a lie will lead to desolation of value and material. This just shows you that it is because we can each choose what we will value yet still seek to have things like the opinions of others as a factor in what you will choose to value. Now we are coming to the present day. There was a time after the second world war that our economy was a production-based economy with 20 %of the jobs were directly connected to the military and munitions production. This put a huge amount of economic strength to any company and leader in the chain of command. It paid dividends to either be in a war or selling munitions and military equipment to other nations. In short, the death of many paid well, and peace was to be avoided so any entanglement we were involved in would not be on a win now basis. In essence the leaders got rich because peace was not common. Playing at war helped deplete the stockpiles and drive the need for new production. The fact it cost the lives of the sons, and daughters, fathers, brothers, etc. was a sacrifice society said was good. Notice the loss was taught to be good rather than go full force into the area and wage complete war to remove the opposition. This was later demonstrated in the war in the middle east desert storm. It only took days and less lives left undefended. It was not politically expedient, and we had been changing from a production economy to a service industry economy which means we depend on others for production, even our agriculture is being bought up and controlled by foreign nations. All because of money that finds it's way to our political leaders. And political parties. So, the approximation of value or money societies answer to feelings claimed more lives, socialists new they would win even if they did not have to fight our nation because men seek things that they think are free or wont cost. As a matter of fact socialist leaders such as Stalin were happy to point that out. That is why they called it a cold war. As socialism has acquired more political stature and even become the platform of a major political party in this country still sacrifice is what they tell people is good, and the churches even support that teaching in spite of the fact that Jesus said point blank he does not require sacrifice. So, you say you are a Christian, but you do not what I said I don't know you. I hope the many people who do not hold their churches accountable to how they conduct themselves by what Jesus said. As I demonstrated in this chapter people give themselves to the idea of the opinions of other people so important it controls what they do. Odd how women could throw their children and themselves to their deaths over a lie yet most people who say they are Christian and work to be like he was. I ask them if they will pick up their cross and follow me. There will be so few. Yet they will give their all for social appeal. I know they will certainly not understand why they are such an adulterous generation. They think that is about sex, it is about adults not keeping their oaths. And other people not holding them accountable for the destruction they are doing. This adulterous generation says they are Christian yet do not do what he said. They say they serve God but only as they define him, which they cannot do, because they serve division not the whole. They choose to put Jesus before the father he served because they could define him as they wanted to. They do not serve the father because they see themselves apart from the father, not what Jesus said," in the beginning I was in my father, my father is in me, and we are one." To them they think it means wielding what they call power or force. Not realizing this would actually make what Lucifer told them true. If God behaved as they, did they would be equal to him, thus making themselves as true Gods. They preach an apocalyptic end because that is what they seek. They forget the word apocalypse really means drawing back the curtain. Because they think force is the only way to create change, they see God as one of them. He is not, so why do they insist on making him that way? To fulfill what Lucifer said. In reality God is a loving father who does not use force except when it comes to the mercy of giving what they seek. Such as in the case of Sodom and Gomorrah, when he gave them the end, they were willing and supportive of by allowing those in their society to mishandle anyone who came to their town. So, all were truly guilty and therefore deserved what came as a natural consequence to their own actions or, failure to act to stop the abuse. Now think about the world today you live in how many nations seek to serve the false God of the abomination that causes desolation, freedom that God gave the individual must be removed so the society can use force to demand obedience. God does not need to use force, society will and always has destroy itself because they do not serve all only the side they choose. God will not send an army they are already here. But he will not use force to be victorious in fact because he is not like you, he will use what you can't imagine, nothing. You see what has power over you. you give it the power, when you stop giving the abusers your power, they will have none. This is what is coming that I saw. Will it be horrible? If you think of yourself apart from or, equal to God I suppose so. However, if you believe as Jesus did you are part of and one with God and you do not have to fear, then like him you will have life everlasting. I know that it is hard to imagine because people die but life is the fathers, but Jesus came to show you truth. But when you have faith or choose the father and the whole, he created you will have the peace even as Jesus did. Now I don't want you to think it will be easy or without fear, while he did not show it, he felt a twinge of that too, "father, why have you forsaken me?" so, while we would like to think and have been told he had no fear, the facts are he was the son of man as well as the son of God. Therefore, for that brief second, he was more the son of man. We are given the freedom to accept and be what we seek, but only for ourselves and our life, that is dominion in your world for you, it does not mean others lives or worlds. I hope by now you can begin to see how the love and mercy of the father will give you what you need to accomplish your needs and choices. If it is to harm others in any way you will ultimately be the one harmed. If it is unintentional, you have the authority to forgive yourself but if you heard and di not do it was intentional. So, you only have yourself to blame, and since you are your own judge, you will pay.

People think of power in the form of might makes right. God uses love to accomplish because it serves all and does not remove value, but rather increases value. And that is who and what he created this place for. True power and authority can not be forced, only shared. We think in terms of power and force rather than energy and change. In Fact, one of the reasons, we cannot limit or name God is because he is all energy of every type we can not even identify or know yet. His various forms of energy causes change as I told you earlier it was the interaction of these various forms of energy that worked to create matter, but there were more forms of energy than we can even know or attempt to define. As a consequence, we use terms like dark matter it is dark now because we know it exist but can't adequately define it. Our acceptance joins forms of our energy with each other that increases the value, I call joy, because it is generally evident in feelings. It is the change and movement that energy produces that we really know as power. We can relate to force because we get to define that form of interaction. Because we remove the purpose or intent from various forms of energy in favor of how we can use them we begin to think of how unlimited we have the power to be. And then we come in confrontation which such things as death. And we glimpse how limited our understanding really is. All of this I am telling you because to see what is going on now you need to understand how it all began and is related to what was. If you are to recognize the truth of what is to come it too is related and connected to what you have allowed to exist in your world now, not the power as you know it but the energy and the purpose of that energy if you are to be part of overcoming what others attempts to use force over you will bring. What I think is horrible is that so much of it comes from man's insistence to replace the reality of the freedom's god gave you with the replacement for the feelings God granted you for dominion so that your society could have dominion over you. Another form of the false God money, have you heard many thinks money equals power? How much of your life have you really given to money rather than make the money work for your goals. Even in that the demand for sacrifice is another way to tell you what others feel you should feel which is why in reality give what you think you should to what you feel because of your feelings and beliefs. The one who will deal without is you if you listen to others and they won't be there to help you when the feelings of how you wasted the value God gave you. Again, people want to tell you what they want you to do not what god wants. In reality as in all thing's god wants you to make it worth more by using it to increase the value of life your own as well as your neighbors. All of these forms in which you have given others the power over your feelings or value of your life. They want to take from you God wants you to make it greater for you and then all.

All of these things are related to what will come. Society will demand money. They will demand the work of your hands and mind, they cannot reward you as they should so they will take from you feelings that give you Joy. That is how their concept of power works. Because this portion of life is tied to time, they can accomplish this, but if you see as Jesus told you that you are one with the father you become no longer tied and limited by time, since he is not limited. This is one of the keys to what will come. The restructuring of power and the world.

CHAPTER 5

Come And See
Deliver Me

I have told you about my vision and the joy of seeing and trying to serve God. Of course, there are many who will say I am not doing it the way they think I should, or worse yet the way their church says it has to be done. I am not here for any particular social group I am trying to share the explanation of the bible that is for all people at all times. The scriptures as we know them were included or excluded from the bible do to social wants and customs. I am called to tell them what I see. If you consider the fact that just about every book in the bible is about how someone saw or interacted with God the father, even Jesus himself. I submit that this book is no different except in it you have received the tools to understand the purpose of all things. It explains consequently the many questions people have about the scriptures and for that matter the right they must choose whatever they have given power too. It is not and never been my purpose to tell you what to believe.

That you must choose for yourself. My purpose is to do exactly what I was told to do, tell them what you see. In that they might be an acceptable explanation of what the scriptures talk to your heart is not my purpose. There are many scriptures that are not in what we consider the bible. There are many different religion's that choose different explanations of who and the nature of God and the world itself. My vision was about what is real, and you can prove it to yourself. Not because of what I said but because you now have the tools to deliver me yourself. It is this significant detail that many churches do not teach. Jesus told you and showed you the way and the truth, but you have to walk it and be as he was serving the father of all for all. That is how he is the savior not just a ransom for your ability to continue sinning and harming each other. In order to fill men's lust for blood and power the churches fail to stress the important part of deliver me which is you choose it and change the way you are.

it is the spiritual vision and journey so full of promise and love, and yet to me so frightening because I want to be a good and faithful servant I do not seek to add to or take from any of the words and meaning that I saw. It was wonderful and frightening as well, because I thought why would they believe me? Instead of seeing just as he was teaching me and showing me answers to questions, I didn't even think about that it would do the same for others. I wondered how important or relevant could this vision be and then it was reminded to me how important was a fisherman's story or a carpenter, or perhaps a shepherd boy? So, you see the truth of the matter is that all are vital because the support and reinforce the father himself. They not only explain the bible they are the bible. I hope after reading this you see as I saw that had this book been available it would have been included. Un fortunately I would have had to meet the same generally unsavory end. That could still happen. While I know the truth about what has been and why I can see the truth about what will be and why, that is what this book is really all about. Now the hard part why I can show you will be is up to you to choose which part you will choose.

This is the part that many have been waiting for the thing they like to think of as supernatural. What I have tried to point out from the beginning what you think of as supernatural is in fact natural. It is related and linked to what came before. It is however like all things subject to the individual. It will happen to all, but some will not see the truth until it quenches their thirst for death and blood. Only then will they realize what they were shown. Again, all of this is contained in the bible and scriptures.it concerns the waking of the dead in God. Many of you have read but can not see the dead in each of you. How long will you let them cry out in each of you for mercy that is the deliverance they desire? The bible says they cry out to God how long, oh lord will you allow this to continue? If you say you are a Christian, I remind you what Christ said and was committed too, I was in my father, the father is in me, we are one. Since you have no mercy of what those who came before you that valued the freedom God gave you, and worship instead the society who can not and will not care what you feel, and believe their sacrifice is enough because it requires nothing from you. Just as Jesus and the many profits and saints sacrifice means nothing and has no value to you because you refuse to care or feel about what they devoted their life too. Thinking you have removed the value they gave their lives for. You will find the past is connected to the future and the present. I am going to show you one way that will happen there will be other ways as well but to most they will begin to have difficulty supporting things like socialism, and the little steps it takes to remove your freedoms will be increasingly bitter. The things they had warned you about will become more apparent to you. You will begin to hear an increase even in the news of supposed supernatural events and the problems that presents to people. Because it talks about the first risen to be the saints and those who died in God, they will not support your need for the accolades of others, they will not support the removal or neglect of the gifts God gave you the individual. They will try to influence you to make better choices and withdraw your power from things that will waste your worth. They will try to influence your teaching the children to try to limit how the lies have been propagated for so long. The result is you will question your own sanity and lose sleep and not find comfort in things you used to take for granted. Because almost all the struggles will be within the individual there is not likely to be much discussion among peers about this because of the questions that arise within you about your sanity. Still the incessant onslaught of people that are afflicted will make the news of course they will try to relegate it to modern stress. That stress originates within you just as your DNA includes their DNA it and they are part of you. If they have found faith, they know they will not die the second death. They know the truth is we not me but all not just the ones who already know. Can you imagine the amount of judgement people will put each other through. Even the church which should have known and been ready to handle what was obviously told you was coming will be afraid to point out the obvious because they did not see it coming and they certainly can not help the individual to deal with it. In fact, I would expect a drastic rise in exorcism. Even that might make the news. It does not matter that they were told it was coming thousands of years ago. Because it did not have a time stamp it can't be real. This is just part of the end of days as we know them, much more is and has been going on and yet to come but again the fact that it does not have a time stamp must mean it is not real. The fact that the scriptures also definitively say that life as usual will be going on won't raise an alarm. In short all of what was promised is and has been going on for a while now. But what about the army in heaven and the return of Jesus to slay the children who do not see? Again, the teachings of men not the vision of God. Why would God behave as men would? He would not and to do that as I have pointed out earlier would make lucifers lies the truth, so where does the church and the Christ come into this? He told you his words then a long time ago and relives them and the meaning of them now. The people who have chosen to love his father as he did and that understand like him, they must be born again not apart from but one with the father each a part that supports and helps all the other parts do what God gave for them to do. It is this sharing together of the individual to accomplish the will of God who is in all that increases God which is why this was created in the first place and the time for learning how to is done the time for doing is now and because every individual who is able will be there and the ones who have chosen to be apart will be, and heaven will be here on earth. Kind of disappointing for those blood thirsty individuals who have waited so long for revenge. But also, kind of joy filled for those who sought to see the fathers will complete and without the suffering, so many people seek, for the other guy I might add because they still don't understand the other guy is me. There are things that will occur that makes this possible. But, in order to understand I will deal with that later.

For now, I want to pray for all including my family and all who know me. I give thanks to our father for showing me what will be and pray that my vision can help others to see they are not apart from God and choose to be one with God and all that he created including each individual. It will be up to them. I say as Jesus did and the other prophets who saw. That since death is it will be only the first death that you have little to no control over that is the realm of this portion and the societies you build and empower here. That power is given by you the gift of life is not subject to your power. Jesus said pick up your cross and follow me, how it got from that to a war here should tell you something about the true motives of men and the churches. For them it seems he would have said pick up your sword and follow me. There will be death but not of the second kind to all who do not choose it. To choose life do not fear the first death. It is going to take that to overcome the power men give to this world. It is the transcendence of this portion.

How long will you seek the blood and death and suffering of each other until you know what causes one to suffer will cause all to suffer? That is the two-edge sword, because it does not mean you are entitled it means what you seek you can achieve and together you help each other overcome but you can not overcome for someone else. Just as you can not make them choose to feel any way unless they allow it. I know you count on fear and pain to accomplish that, but it gets to a point your fear and pain will not overcome what they choose. It is this lie that people rely on and are stunned when it does not work. They assume that they can choose for each other what they think they must feel it is equally a lie and most damaging when they say someone can not do for themselves so you must do it for them. Unless they do as much as they can and try to overcome you will remove all of the value of whatever you do for them without them. This is one of the ways societies can and must fail because it removes the value instead of making it greater it is well known in the bible as, the abomination that causes desolation, this is one of the ways it earns that name. oh I forgot it seems that todays churches again don't talk much about this probably because like the difference between sacrifice and mercy they don't see the importance of knowing. It does not seem relevant to them even though it is prominent in the scriptures or Jesus himself pointed out the importance and need to know. If these are not important to them then the value of life or death is also meaningless to them from the value point of view, and perhaps that is why they feel the authority to judge is their place. Again, this thinking condemns it does not deliver me. Because they teach and seek the loss of any value, they can not understand the truth of value and how the value of all things together raises or increases and makes the joy of the gift of life greater which is what God is, they can not understand each of the many nuances and subtle ways in which that increase occurs. They only understand the increase that they think because it is apart from it creates more loss than any increase it causes. But that is the nature of the abomination so many believe it to be the right thing,

but it candidly causes the exact opposite of Gods will to happen. But all things are included in what God made so, no matter the loss like those who decide to be apart from God they and the less they seek are accounted for and contained.

So now let me ask you what and how are you delivered? Is it

I hope you now see that your thought process and the things you have chosen to value will make you do things that are not right for you or anyone. It is unseen as far as people being aware of why you chose what you did. But normal in that everyone has the ability too. But it is the results of this process they can call supernatural because they really don't understand the truth of what is natural. I have been trying to get people to understand as Jesus told you there is so much more you are capable of, but you believe what others say seem it becomes super natural until you find out you can really do it then for you it is natural. Why is this important? Because all the people Jesus healed knew he could the people who have miracle healings believe it can happen when they don't believe without reservation they are not healed. Because of their doubt so many miss the opportunity to be truly healed. And settle for what is good enough but not everything it could be. in this I am talking about people who have had disease or injury if you do not believe you will be healed you won't, you can make it better by refusing to allow others to tell you what you should be and how you should be functioning and commit to not allowing anything to stop you and doing the best you can with every thing you can. But if you think it can't happen because others say it can't or worse, yet you don't believe enough that it can, you won't be completely healed. What you believe is what you receive. Again, you choose to filter your belief through other people or do you become one with god? It is not easy to have that certainty and keep it but knowing it exists is their reason eventually this is just a portion. Even if you were as blessed as I was and got to see all things and talk with God, it must remain a portion. The reason you are here is to choose for yourself what comes next, will it be life more joyous and abundant, or will you push all away who do not feel what you feel, leaving yourself alone forever.

So now let me ask you, are you delivered because of death or are you delivered because you are living better? Oh, how about do you now understand the first and the second death and it is after the first that you can live greater because you are one and greater than anyone could even imagine. In order for that to happen you must choose and know before the first death.

CHAPTER 6

Come And See
The End Of Days

The end of days as we know it is not the end of time. The contents and things that are contained here are the bread of life more abundant, eat and be filled then raise the joy in your own life and each other's lives. Be full and make the gifts the father has given you greater in every way. Do this as well in memory of the ones who have given their bodies for you. Their death is not a sacrifice if you do not allow it to be forgotten and the value dismissed by the world as we know it today.

I have been telling you of the things I saw on my journey, and how many of them have been part of an ongoing litany of the pursuit of a lie as though they were the truth, which is what the bible says about it being in the last days, however, if you see the speed with which this is destroying all value I believe you must conclude as I saw that it will consume more than we can produce quickly. That will cause worse shortages and greater famines and plagues as well. It will also limit and remove the ability to respond to natural disasters as well. In short, the world as you know it is changing, rapidly. Mans answer has been traditionally to blame others so they can take from them the things they want. However, the things causing these shortages are created by the very people you have given power over yourselves. This is really not new In itself however because the abomination is global the removal of value so out paces the ability for some to replenish it. is on such a scale coupled with the fact that the abomination removes the drive to produce that there is no way to keep things as we knew them. This will eventually cause the need to at least divert attention from what is happening in order to try to placate the people. It is usually done by villainizing a segment of the population which will provide an excuse for war which generally drives the population by spending what they do not have but explaining that the loser will pay. That too is a lie because when you destroy them you remove their ability to repay. The result is always more loss of value but, if you keep the public from seeing this lie, they will usually be compliant. This is usually done through the control of the media. Who controls your media? It does not have to be a government although they are the ones to enforce it. Generally, it is done by whoever controls what the people believe value is. it could be corporations now, at one time and to a large part still today it was the church. Again, a social structure truly controlled by men. However, now the loss is so global, and the people are so diminished by the excessive demand put on them by society they won't tolerate the increased loss of their daughters and son's husbands and wives by war fare it may not be a plausible answer and after the demonstration of desert storm a long-prolonged affair like they have been able to achieve in the past is not very well accepted. This creates a problem the controllers of value and the political leaders reach a point much quicker than they have in the past that the people reject their diversions and begin the process of removing the power they used to give the social organizations. Case in point the us news services on most major channels are not supported by the crowds as they used to be. in other nations the media has lost quite a lot of their people's trust. This leads to the formation of multiple forms of misinformation to be established to keep the people from realizing they are being used. Because the people who are orchestrating much of this is in the background, they choose the most expendable to try to silence the crowd and use their media sources to cover them. For in stance the Catholic church as a pipeline for escaping Nazi leaders, kept hidden for years. The more trusted the more capable of deception. This is one of the reasons that people will finally be ready for a truth that never changes and to understand it is the individual not the group who ultimately has the real power, so now they become more careful about who they give their power too. People talk about conspiracy theories again another way to silence the crowd an attempt to keep them from thinking for themselves. While they may be separate as far as the perpetrators, they are backed by those behind the scenes so that you really should question social media and things that you give authority over yourself too. You can give up you're thinking to someone else, but you will be the ones who feels the results of their plans not them. I know you think this could sound like a conspiracy theory, but I tell you, you have the power and what will come next that I saw as a result of you giving that power to the abomination that causes desolation. Your government and your news will implore you not to invest your thought or interest in what you hear. At the same time their enforcement agencies the police and military will be sent to threaten the peace of any form of protest. The political parties will accuse each other all of this in an attempt to get you to not think for yourself but stay divided. The reality that it is not one or the other but all who are affected and seem to have no where to turn for help will drive what comes next. In stead of being manipulated by one side or the other understand they both need your power to have any power. The more who refuse to give them that the weaker they become. Become as Jesus did do nothing. As he did do not get violent do not struggle with but do nothing. Turn your back on them. Do not fight or even argue with them let them become what they should be too you background noise. Do not give them your feelings in any way. If you are anywhere that someone who is talking about anything other than how to bring all together regardless of race creed color national origin social status political leanings, turn your back on them. If it is a leader on a pedestal or any where that is not talking about how to bring everyone together regardless of their differences turn your back on them if their motorcade passes turn your back on them. It is not anything but sending them the message you will not give them your authority to separate Gods creation. Notice I said Gods creation not Gods children to be a child you must claim the family and the father if you don't you have set your self apart and God loves you so much, he will allow you to get what you want to be apart from. That is mercy not because he chose it but because you chose it. If the news reporter tries to get you to take sides turn your back on them. If the news is playing on tv in an airport or anywhere public turn your back to it or turn it off if that doesn't seem to work fast enough refuse to buy anything that supports them by purchasing commercial space on them and if that does not work refuse to buy anything that advertises on that channel you have the power don't just talk about it use it. Remember it also when you go to the ballot box after all that is the place, they need to control you the most. Remember to hold all people accountable for what they say and do themselves, so if you are in a public gathering your silence will have the greatest volume. If the person next to you tries ti incite violence by shouting obscenities, he is counting on you to hide him. get away from him if they have a weapon and you can't disarm them and turn them over to the police get down and stay down. If anyone gets up and presents themselves as a leader of your group and does not seek ways to resolve the proper issue turn your back on them. If you do not, just like the people of Sodom and Gomorrah you will be guilty as they are. And if you do not put an end to the violence just as dead.

People in the crowd that incite violence regardless of what they say are not behaving as Jesus would or did if you call yourself a Christian act as he would. He never said pick up your sword and follow me, it would not have done good then or now, he did say pick up your cross and follow me. Because though you may face the first death you will gain life forever as he did.

These understandings are important because unless we stop the violence then we will be dead and if we had the chance to and chose not too, we have given up the like he showed you could have. I know this sounds horrible but that is the way people have allowed it to become because they think that by the time it is their time the first death will be done away with by men. At least that is what so many want to believe. In fact our time here is rapidly approaching a point of no return. Because we have chosen to allow the abomination that causes desolation to collect so much of our power that the only way to solve it will be as Sodom's solution ended up being. But I have seen the crowds turning their backs I have seen the horror in the eyes of the media and the political leaders who have used the people's power to enrich themselves. I have seen the slow beginning and the progression of this when the abomination gets to the point there is no joy in life and the people finally understand and pick up their cross and follow knowing that they leave the evil here. And how the people of God finally do what he wanted for them from the beginning and make the gift worth more not to be given or taken away from them by the ones who seek to be apart. This will be an ugly time because it really takes driving the people to desperation to end this lie. It is a perversion of the truth that is the abomination while it appears to sound good the fact that the value of people exercising the freedom to use the gifts God gave them to raise the joy in life and that they could increase the joy and quality of life for themselves and each other without being restricted or forced to do what someone else says is good enough for them. That the people choose because of joy not force removes so much of the power they have allowed to enslave them.

The tiny incremental steps used are getting to have greater ramifications and each removes more joy in life. The parents who have lost their children to this sometimes the children who have lost parents to it are taking their toll. How much is enough? Parents who have children of the age of military service or in the law enforcement community it seems you have lost authority over them they need to understand their own authority so they will not follow illegal orders that will result in more violence and death. They need to understand that yes, they can be afraid but that does not lesson the need to do what is right. Firing into a crowd of civilians is not right. Especially if the crowd is nonviolent and giving up and pointing out the violence inciters. For in what they do they need the same certainty that they have not judged another but saw and held accountable those who judged themselves by what they did. They also must hold their fellow law enforcement or military members accountable to the same judgement. Just as the inciter in the crowd seeks cover by the crowd so too members of law enforcement and military who have judged themselves by what they did need to be accountable. Including any officer who would give the order to fire is guilty. Covering for the guilty only makes you guilty even if only you know the truth. If it were intentional and caused death or harm it must be resolved and forgiven, or it will fester.

As I said what I am trying to put into words here are part of the spiritual vision. Sometimes because

I did not want to see these things. Therefore, they are not as clear to me so long later. These things were particularly hard for me because of the people who we must trust and hope they are of the best character some of them showed the worst. Had it have not been that even during this whole vision I was truly aware that my body was not there so it could not have been a dream. I even asked God why me? Because even in my vision I found this hard to believe or imagine. And if I felt that way why would somebody even believe it. But I am praying thar this time I am doing all he said and telling you what I saw even the parts that worried me at that time and for that matter now. However today I know so much more about how these things came to be even possible and unfortunately probable. Also, many of the events that at that time would have seemed almost impossible happen on a regular basis not only around the world but in this country as well.

The fact that I saw all these things is for me. Also, the fact he told me to tell them what you see is for you. Just as I saw the people around the world will stand up and turn their backs on those who preach division. Will come to be. that people will turn their backs because they are given no option because of the lies and mistreatment of those they gave their power to will happen I wish it were for them as it is for me and was for Jesus when he went to Jerusalem in spite of what he knew what would happen understanding the father wants us all to choose the things he wants for us which is to increase the value of all things he gives us, as he is always increasing and greater. And those who love this life more than him will lose it. So, for me knowing what all this means I have tried to do the best I can to do as he told me. I know there will be many who do not see but I was not called for them. As for me with this work I understand and am ready to pick up my cross and follow him. It will take that readiness and peace to stand up and turn your back but choose life more abundantly when you do. How much peace do you have?

CHAPTER 7

Come And See Armageddon

I have dealt with so much about the end of days, now I will deal with the Armageddon I saw. The war between Gods army and that of man. Will be fought without a shot since it is for the increase of all. The losers will remove themselves because they chose not to be a part of. You could do this as many today is doing thinking there is no God, or you could reject the concept of God because you don't see it the way others have tried to tell you about him, you would be less wrong that way. But if in your heart there is no God you are lost. But the struggle will be real. In order to pick up your cross and follow Jesus to life more abundant you will have to know the father your description of him like mine can not be complete if it where he would not be God. I have told you how the first begin to make their presence known or rise. Although many can't see it but they can not deny if they close their eyes and think of them they are there in some form. Still, those who look for the letter of the word will look for a physical form apart from themselves. They miss the intent of the word. The fact that you will wrestle with the differences in what you think is important and what they thought was important is still a struggle and in order to resolve that struggle you will have to see as my vision showed me from both perspective and from the viewpoint of Value. Because ultimately it is what gave you and them feelings, you may have just allowed different things to establish what you consider a value. Try to remember the world they lived in and saw it will help you to resolve the differences, but remember the truth never changes so take care that the things you are choosing to support yourself are the truth always or you will never resolve the conflict and you will suffer the misery that comes with that. It is energy that cause movement even physical movement so the fact your inner conflict is real should demonstrate the reality of what was said. The dead shall rise. To become something, you will have to deal with. The infirmaries are full of people dealing with their inner conflicts. So, it is very real. The second part becomes disturbing because it talks about how the victims, or the losing side are dealt with. Again, it is the doctrine of men shown in a way they would have understood the judgement day. I believe this will refer to the living who are still in the process of judging them selves by what they said and thought and did that failed to do what the fathers will was for the children. Because the way everything was called into being and all that were given the choice it judges itself by what it chose. Everything judges itself by the result od what it does somethings that do harm still in the end are used to make good. But these are things not with the choice, so they become a matter of perspective. Such as a typhoon or hurricane from some perspectives they are devastating but they also prepare the ground for increase, so it becomes what others do with it. People's choices are independent of what others do. The way true judgement and justice must work the individual is held accountable for only what they did, not what someone else thought or said they did, that is how true judgement works. So, you see in that scenario each of them would come before the father one at a time to review their lives and then they either could plead for forgiveness or mercy and be changed to someone who would forever choose what the father valued, or they would choose to be apart from and be apart. If it were to be done in a day, it is not likely a day as we know it. But like my vision which took less than a day but spanned from before the beginning of time the reference today would not be as we know it. And like my vision I think we judge ourselves through our lifetime and we receive the results of how we judged ourselves at once. As always, I leave that up to your working out what you will believe. The result is heaven here on earth. Where everyone realizes that to help themselves, they must help each other. If we learn to do that, we are ready to find heaven. In my opinion this struggle has always been, and it is not just the unlucky ones left alive that must face it but, like my vision timeless. The final conflict to men must be like all other things subject to others. One of the ways, you can know the truth is it has consequences despite what other men think. It is one of the ways you can try all that is said in this book. It must be that way since it is not something even a group of men could manipulate. The final conflict must be within the individual because the conflict is about value and God gave only the individual to determine their own value by what they will choose to feel about it as a result of what they choose to value. It is not like conflict over property but sharing and joining a form that does not tally its victory or defeat in the loss of property but in value that was never created in the first place. To increase you must add to in this case because we are talking about joy it can not be held in the hand but when created can make you feel like walking on air. As it should be when two people love each other and share their love it makes them feel as though they are walking on air.

What will this struggle look like? As I have already said this struggle while at once hidden yet very real because it will be one of the ways that people have to come to grips with what side they are on, and still understand that in reality there are no sides but one decision is critical for each of them. I think to try to demonstrate this I will use the documented steps of Jesus and how and why he knew what would happen for him in Jerusalem. For him it was his Armageddon. He knew that the power at that time was entrusted to the Jewish church because they refused to understand that there was one God not the different God for different people. Yet Jesus had spent his life talking to the people about the father he knew who was the creator of all. He knew it would not be something that the leaders of the church would approve because they needed to be apart from whatever they felt was less than them in Gods eyes. Even that custom left unchecked was a churches statement that if true limited God. Jesus never taught that or spoke of such things in his ministry he knew that when it came to a confrontation of faith he would not deny the father he knew and that because of the misunderstanding of value and worth the church had grown so dependent upon money and material wealth that it lost sight of true wealth. And that in order to face them he would be required to demonstrate something supernatural that they could not doubt was from God. Since death was the end proof for them, he knew he would die. But he also knew he would survive. Although I doubt if he really knew how or in what form. He had frequently spoken of the prophets before him and the prophesy that told them he was coming said that they would kill him and that the witness would not die. To help you understand I point out to what he said to his accusers destroy this temple I will rebuild it in three days. I believe he was not just quoting what the previous prophets had said but knew they were speaking of him. This is from the many times he was able to spend time with the father, even though others were with him almost constantly he knew and spent time with the father. I would have to guess it was in a similar form to my vision. My body was here but I wasn't. and even as I said my concern and fear was real I can only admire his devotion so that it was only after he was being crucified he showed any doubt father why hast thou forsaken me? It is comforting to me to know that kind of fear was in him as it was in me when I knew what I saw would create the same kind of fear and realization to those who refuse to see. And just like then they will require supernatural evidence to accept as proof. Just as then that kind of activity will only happen for those who believe they can happen. They do not recognize the supernatural downfall of the world around the and the speed with which it is happening. Just as they have not acknowledged the change so drastic in just the last two hundred years, from horse drawn carriage to landing and walking on the moon. The development of the atomic bomb to the supersonic delivery methods today. Still, they do not recognize the end times, famine plagues and pestilence as well as famine. Think of the wealth that has been poured into all of that, still you can't see how those times would not be seen as anything but the end times? Weapons that can destroy the livability of the surface for years. Dead man switches on nuclear systems. Yet they will require that someone who shows them the truth be prepared to show them what they have been blind to. They have grown blind to the supernatural in forms they can't really control, therefore they will require what they can't control. That is why the end has to be in the way I am telling you about because the only supernatural thing they can't really control, or change is what God gave the individual the freedom to decide what they will consider true value, and no one can make the individual change if he decides not to allow it to happen himself. It Is centuries later the same problem exists the ability of the individual not to be misled by the society. Again, the idea of the abomination that causes desolation. It is a shame that people have been taught not to think or reason things out. That the truth comes from society in spite of the photos and videos of the inhumanity of war.

CHAPTER 8

Come And See, Conclusions

The best way for me to tell you what I saw is this. Our father, not your father or my father, who art in heaven, your kingdom, which since you are the creator of all, thy will be done, that all that is in you be one and know your peace and raise your glory. Hallowed be your name, sacred is your name because when we name something we think we can define it, and we can not define or even comprehend all that is you much less limit it by our definition. Thy kingdom come, your kingdom where we are not divided and apart from but, part of you just as our physical DNA with our earthly fathers join us with them. Thy will be done, that you are always more than we can name and define which means as we are part of you, we must be constantly seeking more and better than. On earth even as it is in heaven, here in this physical world you have given us to learn to be greater as you are greater. So, we can live here without division as it is in heaven. Give us this day our daily bread, those things that will nourish us physical and emotional and mentally to do that which you have for us. Lead us not into temptation, do not show us ways we can think to divide or judge each other by our desires which will separate us let us overcome the temptation. Deliver us from evil which is dividing things by what we think. Instead of watching to see how they judge themselves by the results they produce. Forgive us our trespasses, we are here to learn which we know we will make mistakes that if unintentional we know you will forgive us. As we should forgive each other's trespasses or those who trespass against us. Seeing how they judge themselves and not removing the consequences of how they judge themselves because that is how they learn to be one with us and you. For to live as you intended for us thy will be done we will raise the value of all that you have given to make it greater as you are greater, so your will be done here as it is in heaven.

You see this does describe how we are supposed to be and implores God to help each of us see this independently. Just as it has been seen by all those who have been given the sight from the beginning. As in all the things contained in this book they are witness to what Jesus and all of the saints and prophets with sight told you. Directly from their words not what someone said about them. What I saw is the complete embodiment of this and so much more because it does not deny what was necessary for everything to exist, rather it allows you to understand you have the power to pick only for you how much you will participate in. it is not society but the individual that can fulfill the fathers will and raise their value which is always done by increasing the joy they feel which requires they share it with someone who is capable of sharing it to increase the joy you feel and the father feels your feelings because besides you he is the only one capable of knowing your exact feelings because he knows why you chose to feel about what you do. Everyone else guesses unless they have the same feelings for generally the same reasons. It is not enough to just say the words you must understand what they mean and why they are important. Do not take for granted that just because someone knows what they are supposed to say that they really know the meaning of what they say. Because to you it may mean something considerably different. That is why socialism is the abomination that causes desolation. It is not a political statement it is a fact by the results of what it produces and that it can only exist by the removal of the individuals right to freedom given and confirmed by the creation and the creator himself. It is not political it judges itself by what it will always do.

I am not a politician nor a leader of any religion I am the least of those that has seen heaven and experienced the joy and wonder of being with and talking or more appropriately sharing with God. You can believe what you wish, but it can not change what he showed me. And I say try the principles I have contained here and see for yourself. It is the individual God wants to hear from and know what you create as your society is an extension of you. If you divide which is what evil does you try to discount what is required for all things to be or get greater. You make yourself the final arbiter instead of the father who knows the entire truth. Consider these things for your self do not set yourself apart from but be one with Jesus and the father of all. It is your ability to remove yourself that is the second death because it is in keeping with what you chose not what someone else chose for you God so love you he gives you the right to choose and in order for mercy to exist he must allow what you have chosen to occur happen so if you turn your back to him you will be apart not only from him but all that is in him which is everything so you will know the loneliness of true hell. Not because anyone else sent you there. So, I ask you who do you believe? Men or however you know God himself, not what men say which is the limited God they can define?

I hope you will take the time to know your answer. As for me I am who he called me to be with you and him one which is what Jesus taught and why they killed him. I am the least of them a witness to them.

www.ingramcontent.com/pod-product-compliance
Lightning Source LLC
Chambersburg PA
CBHW051548120626
46551CB00013B/1428